THE LEVOLUTION

*An evolution for women who have been
Blocked, Broken and Stuck!.*

April D. Graham

Copyright © 2020 April D. Graham

All rights reserved.

No part of this book may be reproduced or transmitted in any form or by any means, electronic or mechanical, including photocopying and recording, or by any information storage and retrieval system, without permission in writing from the publisher.

Printed in the United States of America

ISBN: 978-0-578-80328-9

LEVOLUTION

Verb: the process where some women Level Up, and other women Level Up and Evolve

DEDICATION

I dedicate this book to ALL women. It is for those of you who find it difficult to cope. You struggle, suffer and have been stuck for so many years. Don't give up! Hold on, beautiful! Your help is here! Also, the Levolution is for us, who are called "strong women." We who endure, overcome obstacles and persevere when we secretly cry silent tears. Yet, we pull ourselves up when people and situations try to hold us down. We manage every day to be everything to everyone, except ourselves.

    I am you

TABLE OF CONTENTS

FORWARD 1

ACKNOWLEDGMENTS 3

1 LEVEL UP BY REALIZING THAT SH%@ HAPPENS 6

2 LEVELING UP FROM PAIN THAT YOU WERE TOO YOUNG TO CAUSE 13

3 LEVELING UP WHEN YOU ARE LOST 19

4 LEVELING UP WHEN YOU ARE LONELY 24

5 LEVELING UP WHEN YOU ARE LAUGHED AT 32

6 YOU ARE LOOSED TO LEVEL UP 45

7 LOOK UP TO LEVEL UP 50

8 LEVEL UP AND LEAD 56

9 LOOK FIERCE WHILE LEVELING UP 60

10 THE LEVOLUTION 69

11 LEVEL UP –IDENTIFY YOUR SH%T 74

12 LEVEL UP –OWN YOUR SH%T 80

13 LEVEL UP –DEAL WITH YOUR SH%T 88

14 LEVEL UP –GET OUT OF YOUR SH%T... 95

15 LEVEL UP –GET INTO YOUR SH%T 101

16 LEVEL UP –BE CONFIDENT IN YOUR SH%T................................. 107

17 LEVEL UP –BE UNSTOPPABLE IN YOUR SH%T 116

18 LEVEL UP –BE UNDENIED IN YOUR SH%T 121

19 LEVEL UP –BE UNBREAKABLE IN YOUR SH%T........................... 129

20 LEVEL UP – CONCLUSION 134

ABOUT THE AUTHOR – SHE IS THE SH%T 141

FORWARD

If there is ever a time when we need to be real with God and real with ourselves, it is now! In this new era, new decade, and new season, I believe God wants to see us all launch out to the fulfillment of Purpose. The Levolution movement has come along for such a time as this!

Many of us have been trying all we can to walk in Purpose & Destiny. Only to find that we have only been able to go so far. We often feel stunted, stuck, hindered and unable to forge ahead and are not fully cognizant of the reason. We often blame it on the system, our family, our finances, our race, our past or even the devil. Even though some of these things may play a role in influencing your circumstance, ultimately, it is up to you and how you deal with it. In other words, if you are ready to go to that next level to cite a principle by this author, "It's time to *level-up* and *evolve."* When you realize that you have been at a certain level for so long and want more, it is time to *level up*! You have the power within you to overcome and forge ahead into purpose and destiny. Sometimes we are our worst enemy because we refuse to "look in the mirror."

The *Levolution* book and series is very timely. The author has used her experiential knowledge of change and transformation through her life struggles and triumphs. She is "An overcomer by the blood of the Lamb and word of Her testimony." (Revelations 12:10) This book will give you practical tools and spiritual principles to help get you to the next level in life. This might require facing your demons, processing your hurt, pain, and shame. It may require God's grace to help you in the forgiveness process. It may require being real with where you are and deciding to 'level up" and look up to the Hills from whence comes your help (Psalms 121). Level up and receive the *Levolution* to a life of peace, prosperity, wholeness and fulfillment.

I am excited to endorse this book and know that the thought-provoking language and examples cited will reach you right where you are and further propel you into excelling to the fulfillment of purpose. As you read this book, you will begin to take a hard look at yourself, your past, present and future.

Please read and re-read again and again until the mindset shift occurs. You will not regret this investment into your glorious future.

Enjoy & be Blessed

Minster Darlene Davis-Hord, Life Purpose Coach

Director of Daughters of Zion-Women of Destiny Mentorship Organization

ACKNOWLEDGMENTS

First, I acknowledge my Master, my Messiah and the one I call El Shaddai—the Almighty God. I trusted YOU even when I could not trace YOU, and you have shown me, time after time, that YOU never left me and that YOU were faithful to fulfill your word. Next, to my wonderful husband, Maxie. I am so grateful for the love and support that you give me. Because of you, I exhaled, and for this, I will forever love you. Thank you for loving me through my flaws and telling me how fierce I am every chance that you get. To my bonus baby, Kania, you have been a part of my life as one of my own, and you make me proud to be your stepmom. I will always love you. To my lovely girls, Ramona and Zaria, you are my everything. Every hour I work, every class that I take, everything that I do, and every day that GOD opens my eyes, I love you more than you will ever know! To my champions and cheerleaders (my friends, family and framily), thank you for always supporting and encouraging me.

I am grateful for all of your support, encouragement, and love.

You are my WHY!

"You are the daughter of the King!

Let's make them regret that they ever doubted that you are Royalty!"

April D. Graham

WELCOME TO THE LEVOLUTION!

The movement for real women with real problems who are ready to

Level-Up, Look Up and Lead while looking Fierce doing it

1 LEVEL UP BY REALIZING THAT SH%@ HAPPENS

WELCOME TO THE LEVOLUTION!

This is not another self-help book. This is not another book about encouragement and motivation. This is a mindset, a mission, and a life-long movement to become the very best version of YOU. Point blank! The Levolution is about Leveling Up! More importantly, although it is about Leveling Up, it is also about Evolving! This is a process where you will be Leveling up physically, emotionally, spiritually, and in all areas of your life.

Here's what I know for sure, any woman can Level Up. It's real simple to do. Yet, few women actually evolve. Hence, through The Levolution process, I challenge you to not only Level Up but to Level Up and Evolve by changing a faulty mindset, discovering your personal mission for your life, and joining the movement to do more and become better!

Let me warn you. This book is not for the thin-skinned, easily offended, fence straggling little girls who are not really sure if they are willing to make the commitment with themselves. This is for real women with everyday problems that have been stuck in their shit*uations* way too long and are ready to Level-Up, Look Up and Lead while looking fierce doing it.

I penned this book as a guide for getting out of your situation. Let me be clear, what I really wanted to say is, it's for (GETTING OUT OF YOUR SH#%T), but as a wholesome Christian woman (laying my prayer cloth on my lap), I didn't want to offend anyone by using cuss words.

So, throughout this book, please allow me to be an "imperfect Christian" and use shit*uation*. Yes, this book is for getting out of your "shit*uation*"!

With this being said, I was inspired to write this book for non-believers, new believers and for mature believers who can sift through the innuendos and get this message. The fact of the matter is, whether you are Jew or gentile, a slave or free, you are in a shit*uation,* or you will be faced with a shit*uation*.

Here is my disclaimer—I am an in your face, say it like you mean it kinda gal. Sometimes, I lack tact, and my words are sharp (as a dagger), and I say it exactly as I feel it.

No cutting corners, no babysitting, and darn sure is not accepting any excuses. So, if you have the mental fortitude, a "hell can't stop me" attitude and are ready to serve an eviction notice on your procrastination, your past and your pain, get ready to Level Up!

I have several college degrees, but I have also earned a Masters in Overcoming Obstacles and my Bachelor's Degree in Bouncing Back from Setbacks.

Unfortunately, these are the credentials that I treasure the most. You see, Surviving the Pain was not offered at the university. It wasn't on the syllabus nor located in the course catalog. So, by way of life experiences, I am a certified, bonafide Bounce Back Queen. As you read through the first few pages, I want you to really connect with my story to understand who I am so you can understand why I am here writing this book today.

After reading that intro, you may be wondering, is this right for me, or can I really change my shit*uation*? I am here to tell you without a shadow of a doubt, YES, YOU CAN! I say that with every breath in my body and everything in me because it was me. I am her (with my hand raised)—brokenness, insecurities, neglect, divorce, rejection, molestation, and abuse is my story.

This book is for grown women. By Google's definition, adult females who have been locked up and lost in their circumstances. For those who have yet to realize or come to terms with the fact that they are entangled, entrapped and enslaved to a poor mindset, a method of poor choices and bad habits, and a morgue of shit*uations*.

It is for "grown women" who, year after year, have not managed to pull themselves out of their pit of problems. In fact, you have settled for the same things, at the same place, with the same people, all at the same time. Let's pause so that you can process this for a moment!

P – process what I've said thus far

A – acknowledge that you are in some shit*uations*

U – understand where I'm coming from

S – start to see yourself as free

E – excuse yourself from the procrastination, and let's get started

My Sister, I know that might have cut you deep. I forewarned you that this journey would not be easy. However, I'm here to guarantee you that if you allow this book to speak to your spirit, if you can get the words LEVEL UP and EVOLVE down in your soul, YOU WILL GET FREE! I repeat, YOU WILL GET FREE!

Let me be clear, I write this book not to condemn or judge you (GOD knows I have gotten myself in some shit*uation*s). Hopefully, you will read my story and become so encouraged and inspired that you, too, receive your breakthrough from the barriers that have been holding you back.

This book is a process. It is not intended for you to scan through the pages, highlight a few keywords and then store on your bookshelf. This book is meant to serve as your go-to guide, your go-to for strength, for strategies and your go-to manual for renewing your mind. Its purpose is to serve as your bible of beliefs. Your belief first, in GOD (or who you recognize as your higher power). Then, your belief in YOU. This book should be your collection of short stories where you are constantly going through levels until you reach your goals.

Now that I have given you the tough talk and we have gotten the feel sorry for myself part out of the way, are you ready? Are you ready to Level Up? I am talking about making changes in every area of your life. Leveling Up in your mindset, Leveling Up in your finances, Leveling Up in your career, Leveling Up in your home and in the way you walk and talk.

You see, The Levolution is your life's solution for evolving to become the best version of YOU! It will require a shift in your mindset. It is a mission that everyone will see that you have been there, done that and as the saying goes, got a t-shirt to prove it. It's about going from surviving to thriving. The Levolution is a movement for showing up and becoming the author of your own story. One who gets to write in a chapter that says – I DID IT, I LEVELED UP and I EVOLVED!

"Childhood trauma can lead to an adulthood spent in survival mode, afraid to plant roots, to plan for your future, to trust, to let joy in.

It is a blessing to shift from surviving to thriving. It is not simple but there is more than survival."

Dr. Thelma

CHILDHOOD SHI*TUATION*

2 LEVELING UP FROM PAIN THAT YOU WERE TOO YOUNG TO CAUSE

I was born April Denise Mosley on July 21, 1970. My parents divorced when I was around 4 years old, so my memories of Ben are short and sour. I remember him being semi-active in our life before the age of 8, and then he was a part-time dad who showed up sporadically around 16 years of age. I am the middle child of two sisters. Sadly, my childhood memories of my mom are equally daunting. Although she was the custodial parent, our "visits" with her were also part-time. Let me explain.

My mommy, two sisters and I lived in a middle-class neighborhood in Miami. My mom was either working or "partying," leaving her three girls to rely on themselves or (thankfully) the Hispanic neighbor who would notice her disappearance and bring over food. When my mom was not working, she would leave us home alone. Mom would literally be gone for days. Leaving me feeling rejected, neglected, abandoned, and for my little sister and I, abused. My baby sister and I would endure starvation, physical beatings, and emotional turmoil until mom returned from her extended stays, only to go through another round when she left again. By her own admission, my mom was an addict. She was addicted to drugs and alcohol, and that is what fueled her absence.

One day, walking home from our elementary school, we arrived home to find all of our things on the front lawn. We were evicted! Yes, put out of our childhood home. I remember being so embarrassed and ashamed because of the stares from the neighborhood kids and the passers-by. The feelings I experienced while bagging our things in trash bags make me sick to my stomach to this day! For me, I think that this was the birth of my emotional eating, insecurities, and low self-esteem. It was here, at this moment, that I enrolled in "Life University" to pursue my AA Degree in survival.

Our eviction relocated us and caused us to live with an aunt. Before you say that we were blessed in finding shelter and before you praise the family member for taking us in, hold your applause! This was a really difficult, horrifying, and challenging experience for me. Don't get me wrong, I'm grateful because I believe my aunt was really sincere in giving us a place of refuge, but her sincerity quickly turned tragic.

During this time, my mom was heavily into her addiction, and her extended stay-away became more frequent. My little sister and I were familiar with the routine, so her absence was no stranger to us. However, this time, something different happened when she left.

Mom was leaving for her "extended stay," as she often did. On this particular night, I remember her instructing us to place the bottle behind the door, so when he entered the room, the bottle crashing to the floor would supposedly awake us. Well, the bottle did not wake me because we later discovered that he was entering the bedroom through the window. My cousin, the sexual predator, would break into our bedroom and sexually molest me. The memory of him laying on top of me (makes me want to puke) is still vivid in my mind.

After fighting him off me, I screamed, yelled, and ran to tell my aunt. She yelled at him, and I remember standing there with this blank stare on my face as she admonished me, "don't wear short shorts around him" (sorry, I am pausing here to shake my damn head).

Like, who says this? Who asks a child not to wear short shorts in front of their son, who is a sexual predator? At the onset of these words falling off her lips, I remember feeling unsafe and unstable as a child. Her words confirmed the voices in my head that were already saying to me that no one cares, no one listens, and no one is going to save you.

The damage, disappointment, and despair that I experienced in our childhood home had followed me to this new address. So, here I was, moving from an unhealthy environment into an even more unhealthy environment.

At this point, I was trying to navigate life as a young child dealing with an absent dad, a neglectful mom, physical abuse, emotional abuse, coupled with sexual-harassment and molestation.

I officially became a teenager and was enrolled at the local

Middle School. I remember thinking to myself—maybe someone will help me here? Is this a place that I can run to? Will I be safe? My answer came quickly, and the answer was HELL, NO! It turned out that a male teacher, who presented himself to the girls as a trusted father figured, lured me into his room one day and fondled me. I remember standing there as he caressed my genitalia. The sad and sick part about it was that I had grown to accept it, and although I was shaken, I was not shook.

As the days went by, I wondered if I should tell anyone? I struggled with if it even mattered. Heck, when it happened from the uncle, cousin, and uncle's friend, nothing happened when I told on them. So, I kept quiet. No one ever found out "our little secret." Get this, he is now a prominent and "respected" member of the community. Yes, you read it right…a "PROMINENT" member of the community.

Once again, I was automatically enrolled in the classes of life, and at this point, it was extremely challenging, and I was failing miserably. This started my journey to earning a Bachelor's degree in Bouncing Back.

Neglected by mom, abandoned by dad, molested by a cousin, teacher, uncle, and family friend. Sexually assaulted by a family friend, rejected by my peers, and physically abused by a caretaker. Whew, and my kids ask me why I am "so strong."

During this time, my only method for Leveling Up was to look for attention, solicit affection, and seek acceptance. That's what I wanted. That's what I needed. Guess what, that's what I found!

"You cannot heal what you do not reveal."

Brandi Jefferson-Motley

TEEN SHI*TUATION*

3 LEVELING UP WHEN YOU ARE LOST

I was off to high school, home of the mighty chiefs. I was taller than many of the boys, curvier than any of the girls, awkward, broken, and desperate for love and attention. In my desperation, I found a family in a local girl gang. We would fight with other gang rivals and were truant from school, drinking alcohol, trafficking drugs, engaging in promiscuous behavior, and other things that unruly teen girls could get into.

I yearned to belong and to be loved, and "my new family" and my boyfriend (older man) was available to give it to me freely. For once in my life, someone accepted me, paid attention to me and supported me. It was dangerous, it was toxic, and I was in the most unhealthy shit*uations* possible for a young girl.

Nonetheless, I did not care. My only desire was to be accepted and loved, and I got what I wanted.

At the age of 17, I graduated from high school (by the skin of my teeth), and the following week, I decided to move out into an apartment with two of my cousins. It is 17-year-old me, my 18 and 19-year-old cousins, on our own, navigating life with no guidance and supervision. Needless to say, we did any and everything that young, unruly, and undisciplined young ladies could do.

It is 1988, and I reiterate, I turned 17 and moved out of the house I stayed with my mom and sisters. Finally, my 18th birthday came, and I was wild, out of control, promiscuous, and to make matters worse, I find out that I am pregnant. Yes, you read it right, I got pregnant.

After having an abortion just a few weeks prior, I decided to give birth to this child. Now, you can add teen parent and welfare recipient to my resume. I became seriously ill during this pregnancy so much that it caused me to become bed-stricken and unemployed. Damn, that was some pregnancy. So, I was forced to move back with my mom and sisters. Here again, I am thrust back into the environment of my mom's drug and alcohol abuse and physical altercations with my older sister. Once again, I am in a shit*uation!*

Looking back, I realize that getting pregnant might have saved my life. As an eighteen-year-old pregnant teen who was lost, I realized that I needed to Level Up or I would repeat and replicate what I had experienced growing up. I frequently cried and thought that I did not want to bring a child into this world to experience life as I had as a young girl. I became obsessed with what it was that I could do so that my child would have a better life.

Then one day, I made a commitment to my unborn child, and I vowed that I would do everything in my power to make sure she would be okay.

The majority of my family were either high school dropouts or high school graduates at best. Not to mention that they too struggled with drug addiction for many years as well. We were close-knit and had a tenderly toxic love for one another, if that makes any sense. During this time in my life, we would gather regularly as a family unit. However, it was for the sole purpose of the adults coming together for their 'get high parties.'

So, without any model of "success," I created a "successful" life by relying on what I read or what I saw in other families, on television, or what I could glean from books and magazines that I would read.

I was lost as a young girl, but I was determined as heck as a teenage mom. So, out of that determination, I Leveled Up and enrolled myself in the local community college.

> *"Freeing yourself was one thing; claiming ownership of that freed self was another."*
>
> *Toni Morrison*

YOUNG ADULTHOOD SHIT*UATION*

4 LEVELING UP WHEN YOU ARE LONELY

The father of my child and I made the decision to provide stability for our child. So we decided to move in together with the hopes of being a family for her. Both of us were from a single-parent home, so we knew all too well about the struggles of parenting alone. During this time, I was really working hard to remove myself from all the harmful people, places, and things in my life.

I wanted more for Ramona (my child) and better for me. My soul was searching for a way out. A comfort. Approval from my college-attending friends and genuine acceptance from my two-parent household peers.

I didn't grow up in the church, so I didn't really know anything about this GOD that people would talk about. However, I decided to visit my friend's family church. I remember sitting in the Sunday service thinking that something feels new, different and unlike anything that I had experienced in the past. The church services made me feel warm and safe. I could literally feel the hairs on my arms raise when I would attend.

The people would be dancing, singing, rejoicing, and crying out to this GOD, and the sanctuary would feel electrifying. So, I wanted to explore this "good feeling" more and more. I began attending the church regularly and having these experiences each time that I would visit.

Until finally, I Leveled Up and decided that I needed to give my life to Christ. I joined the Church, and for the first time in my life, I got baptized at twenty-five years old.

I started my journey in Christianity. I began reading scriptures, attending bible studies, and going to church conferences. I surrendered to a higher power and submitted my will to an Almighty God. I stopped doing some of the things that I was doing and going to some places that I would go. My friends would say that I was acting funny. I couldn't rely on anyone else to help me, guide me or lead me spiritually. Therefore, I trusted my gut, and I got saved. It was me and my GOD from here on out.

Considering my "new life" with my newly found Jesus, you would think that I would find my escape from my troubles during these times. That was certainly not the case. Actually, it turned out to be some of the most challenging times for my 25-year-old self.

Here I am, on this journey of discovering Jesus. I'm finding confidence in myself. I'm in college, married, and life for once is stable. Little did I know or ever imagined that adulting with my new husband would nearly break me. Wow, I had gotten myself into a shituation. I had no idea that the weekend I say I DO, my husband #1 would transform into some kind of evil that I am convinced was used by the devil to destroy me mentally and emotionally.

He started (or should I say, he became open) in having multiple affairs. Who the heck gets married, and two weeks later, your spouse is taking secret phone calls in the bathroom and staying out to wee hours in the morning? What newly-wed stays out late nights and then says, "don't question me, I am grown"? Mine! Subsequently, verbally and emotionally abusing their new bride? NO, LIKE REALLY, who the heck does this?

Needless to say, this toxic, abusive and unhealthy relationship lasted through the course of over 17 years with this guy. He would curse me, throw things and break my valuables when something was said or done that he didn't approve of. If I cooked a meal that he didn't want or didn't like, he would hurl the entire pot of food across the room. If I asked him questions that he didn't like, he threw something. If I gave him answers that he didn't like, he threw something. It was certain every day that I would be called a name, witness a wall being punched, microwave smashed or verbally assaulted either via text messages or outbursts upon entering the door from work.

I remember the horror from one day when I called him from work and asked about an unknown charge on our bank account at a beauty supply store. The mere fact that I questioned him sent him into a rage. I came home to our master bathroom being destroyed (the place where I would go to de-stress, soak, and unwind). Let me add, during this time, we lived in a huge two-story home, and the bathroom was massive, and he literally destroyed it! In a rage, this guy vandalized every square foot in the bathroom. He found every glass bottle in the kitchen (plates, drinking glasses, ketchup, salad dressings, hot sauce, etc.) and threw it against the mirror and floors in there. He threw food, flour, sugar and smashed the cabinets. The bathroom was in such shambles with food and glass everywhere, I had to pack up my kids and take them to stay in a hotel for days.

As if his temper tantrums and angry outbursts weren't enough to mentally drain you, he would engage in multiple affairs and dared me to ask about his suspicious behavior. He even fathered a child with his adulteress and cursed me out for confronting him about it. Not even then did I leave my ex-husband.

The day of my breaking point had finally come. I was finally over it and decided to leave him. It wasn't the late-night outings. It wasn't because of the verbal abuse and violent tantrums. It wasn't because he fathered a child during our marriage. It was not even the fact that he would call me names like "fat bi%*h" and "wide load" because I was seriously overweight.

My breaking point came when I discovered that he was having another affair. However, this time, it was with a woman he was cheating with when we were dating. Can you believe that the same woman he cheated on me with when I was his girlfriend was the same woman he cheated with while I was his wife?

So, throughout our 15-year marriage, he maintained this

emotional and physical relationship with this woman. To add insult to injury, we looked so much alike that often, I would be mistaken for her and vice versa. I hated this woman because I knew she had a place in his heart, and he knew that I despised her, but obviously, he could care less.

I finally got the courage to leave this shit*uation*. I was married to this man for so many years, but I was lonely. It was as though we were married but living single. I was getting no affection, little attention and minimal support from this marriage. I was miserable and lonely. I was hurt, but I refused to be held back! I had to make a decision to walk away from a relationship I was in for nearly 20 years. The things my ex #1 DID to me, crushed me; but the things he SAID to me, broke me down!

You see, the truth be told, I was able to move past the affairs and the child he had with his mistress. But I could never get those harsh names that he called me out of my head. I remember balling in my bed, wondering how in the heck did I allow HIS words to shape MY reality???

You know how? Because I had low self-esteem and lacked confidence and I was broken. One day I came home, and just like that, I said, it's over. I picked up the phone and called a divorce attorney.

I needed to Level Up, and that's exactly what I did. I Leveled Up by working on me—my mind, my body, and my spirit. I changed my mindset. I had to denounce every word curse that he had spoken over me. I started de-programming all of his horrible words and the negative self-talk that had seeped into my veins. I would declare who GOD says I am and speak positive affirmations over me daily.

I sought counsel from my pastor and from Darius, a spiritual leader in my life. I would hear and process their perspective. Their support would console me and encourage me to get healed and do everything I could to become healthy mentally, physically and spiritually.

I worked so hard on shifting my mindset from seeing myself as a victim to that of a victor. I refused to feel sorry for myself any longer. I would become intentional with daily affirming my worth, and I had to purge all of the negative downloads, spirits and soul ties that he had deposited into my soul and spirit.

I Leveled Up in my body. As an emotional eater, I had gained weight to over 315 pounds. I was so heavy, and my weight was so depressing that I elected to have cosmetic surgery. The surgery allowed me to lose 50 pounds, and then I hired a trainer. I would meet with him for 5 am workouts and commit to training three days a week. I became disciplined in my diet and would be conscious about what I would eat. Finally, I would push myself like crazy because I had become this person I hated when I looked in the mirror.

I Leveled Up, and I became more spiritual and connected to GOD. I would do a daily early morning prayer and meditation ritual to get in the right alignment to hear from the spirit. I was working hard and receiving promotions at work. I was watching the power of GOD move in my life. I was empowered. I was confident, and I finally made the decision that I was going to be happy and free.

So I thought.

"It is a courageous act to just be with whatever is happening at the moment – all of it, the difficult as well as the wonderful."

Eileen Fisher

GROWN WOMAN SHIT*UATION*

5 LEVELING UP WHEN YOU ARE LAUGHED AT

I remember the day I met husband number #2. Ouuu weeee! Those brown eyes. He was tall. He was handsome. He was charming. He was charismatic. He was a gentleman, and lo and behold, HE WAS A "CHRISTIAN" MAN!

I convinced myself that HE was the one. Yes, girrrrlllll, I just knew it was HE, who was sent by GOD. The man that I had been praying about and the one that I use to dream of. We were compatible. We were abstinent—"he loved me" (so he said he would wait). We would go on nice dates and had amazing chemistry.

We would talk for hours and hours on the phone. He was a manly man. He took care of all the things that I believe that a man should take care of. He was a praying man; he was a providing man, and he was a protecting man. He had to be the one. The feeling and physical touch that he gave me was unlike any man that I had ever experienced. He would make love to me mentally long before it was physical. Our romance was burning hot. I was convinced that HE was the one.

We met and dated for six months, and then he proposed. Six months after he proposed, we got married. He moved quickly and moved in even more quickly!

He would say that he did not want to risk losing me, and truth be told, I did not want to risk getting lost. It was something about ex #2 that was flattering, and I could not get enough of him or how he made me feel. Nevertheless, ex #2 and I got married, and soon after, those brown eyes started to look red, and that bright smile was now more of a smirk. Unbeknownst to me, my love story was shaping up to be more like a horror movie.

Soon after the I DO, the representative was slowly becoming his authentic self. He became open with his heavy alcohol drinking, and the money he spent while wooing me was no longer available. He was very controlling and strategically worked to isolate me from my friends and family. He would use his "bible psychology" and tell me things like GOD says I should not do this and do that. Oh yeah, he knew the bible back and front (allegedly, he was an ordained Pastor)

He wanted me to himself and refused to even share me with my children. He had to know my every whereabout. His personality was shifty, and his thinking and mindset was warped. Nonetheless, I was quite smitten by him, so I was all in.

One workday, we were getting in from work and settling into our usual weekday routine. He started complaining about body aches. I did what any good wife would do. I massaged him, relaxed him, and catered to his needs. These complaints continued throughout that week, becoming increasingly worse. Each day, he got worse and would come home and complain. It became a daily thing that he would come home, communicating that he was not feeling well. Then, I visibly notice a decline in his health. I'm talking about rapid weight loss, weakness in his muscles and a change in the sound of his voice.

When the weekend came, we prepared to attend my friend's big event. Despite not feeling his best, he said he would press his way and go as his show of support. I am excited about the party, so I headed out Saturday morning to the mall to find the perfect shoes for my sexy dress that I would be wearing that night. I was so excited about that night because he always made me feel special when we went out. I was walking through the mall, energized and thrilled with all of the variety of shoe choices. AND THEN IT HAPPENED! I receive the phone call that, in an instant, literally changed my life. It was that day, that time, and that phone call that I went from being a Newlywed to being a Nurse.

I answered the phone, and it is ex #2 on the other end. He sounded fragile, his voice was feeble, and he was panting, struggling to breathe. I asked him what was wrong, and he told me that he had just called 911 because he was having chest pains and shortness of breath. At this point, I am in a panic and crying frantically.

I arrived at Memorial Regional Hospital, and the Doctor informed me that he needed to be transported to another hospital. She stated that he was exhibiting all the symptoms of a heart attack, but his blood work and test results indicated otherwise. For this reason, he needed to go to the Heart Institute for a more comprehensive exam.

Now, I was perplexed about what happened, overwhelmed by everything that was going on, and exhausted with the thought of my new responsibility of being a nurse and caretaker. As if that wasn't enough to deal with, ex #2 was admitted and was hospitalized for over a month without a diagnosis. Imagine having a full-time, stress-filled day job and then rushing out to the school because my daughter was misbehaving and frequently suspended and then rushing to the hospital to care for my husband.

After having multiple tests performed and observations by various specialists, my ex #2 was finally diagnosed with a rare illness. The disease was so rare that only 10 cases existed in the entire state of Florida. I felt as though my life ended at that moment of the diagnosis. He was diagnosed with this horrible and rare disease; I was struggling with an unruly teen, and I was an Assistant Principal at one of the most challenging schools in the school district.

My ex became increasingly worse by the day. My teen became increasingly rebellious, and my job became increasingly stressful. I was alone. I was overwhelmed, and I was extremely frustrated. As if life could not get any more difficult, it did.

My ex #2 was in and out of the hospital, and I had to transport him to several specialists and multiple doctor's appointments. I had NO ONE to help me balance my life, and there was not anyone to shoulder this responsibility. Not to mention, my boss at the time was down my throat and on my back for my now "mediocre" work performance. My home had shifted to a single-income household, and with every burden there was, I was made to bear them alone.

I felt life at this point for me was non-existent. I experienced life like I was literally the walking dead. My body was tired and beat down. My mind was barely functioning. My spirit was downtrodden, and my soul was in distress. Meanwhile, to add insult to injury, our home was foreclosed, car repossessed, and bank account depleted. Things had gotten so bad that I came home one day to the lights, cable and water all disconnected at the same time.

My husband's health was declining quickly, and I needed to make some decisions quickly. This was the moment in my career where I knew that I had to pivot. I was forced to choose between my sick husband, who needed full-time care, or my position as an Assistant Principal (who was up for a promotion). I chose to resign from my career and care for my husband.

I decided to find a small childcare center and pursue entrepreneurship. Imagine having little money to your name and trying to start a business. So now, I have a sick husband, a disobedient teen, a new business, a foreclosure, a repossession, and a mother-in-law (zipping my lip on the mother-in-law because that story is for the next book); let's just say that I am still dealing with the pain and anger from this person.

For seven years, I endured what I thought was a personal hell. I felt abandoned by my friends and isolated from my family. I had NO ONE! I repeat, NO ONE! When I would lay on my closet floor screaming and crying, NO ONE! When I would get the calls from my daughter's school that she was suspended again, NO ONE! When we had to cash in the coins from the coin jar to pay for food and gas, NO ONE!

When I would only get 3-4 hours of sleep in a twenty-four-hour day, NO ONE! When I had to work at the childcare center for 12 hours and then rush home to feed and bathe my ailing husband, NO ONE! When I had to endure being married with no sex (for over 6 years) and no support, NO ONE! When I was made to look into the barrel of his gun, NO ONE!

I was mocked by my family. I was laughed at and talked about by my friends. They would make snide remarks thinking I was isolated because I thought I was all of that with my new man. Little did they know that I was isolated because I was struggling, barely surviving, and embarrassed and ashamed about my shit*uation*.

One day, amid my dark pit, I had an epiphany. I realized that I was losing my daughter. She was acting out more and more. The more I dedicated my time to my husband, the more distant and disobedient she became.

One day in my defeat, depression and despair, I decided to shift my time and attention to her. I started making her the priority. I would come home and attend to her needs first. I would spend more time talking with her and interacting with her in the home. This made my ex #2 furious.

Although there was not much more that I could do for him, he wanted every ounce and every moment of my time and attention. Even if it meant sitting in the room and watching him groan and gasp for air. Prior to choosing to redirect my attention, I would literally get into an argument with him if I greeted her first when I got home from work.

Imagine living in these conditions. I have a start-up struggling business, a sassy 16-year-old, and a mean, selfish, sick spouse. Oh, and let me add, he became increasingly mean, angry and bitter as his health continued to decline.

He would curse me (he was a certified cusser) when things were not as he wanted them to be or if I gave my child too much attention. The little strength that he did have, he would use it to antagonize my child and verbally harass and curse me.

One day, all hell broke out in the house. My daughter wanted to hang out with her friends at the afterschool event. I told her that she could only go if her room was cleaned up prior to leaving for school. She leaves for school, and my ex #2 decides to verify that she had done what she was told.

Could you believe he could barely walk and needed a cane and walker to move about throughout the house? But this particular day, he made his way to my daughter's bedroom to see if she had cleaned up and folded her laundry like I had instructed her to do. (keep in mind that he was deathly ill).

He was not convinced that she did it. This man managed to inspect the room and search underneath the bed. You read it right; he used his cane to lift the covers off the bed. He found that she hid the laundry underneath her bed, and he actually took pictures to prove it. Well, you probably guessed it—THAT DIDN'T GO WELL WITH ZARIA!

Between her screaming and crying from a meltdown and him literally gasping for air through the curse words, I was nearing a mental breakdown.

The pain was unbearable, unimaginable, and unfathomable. (I am teary-eyed as I write this). I cried and cried, prayed, and prayed that Jesus would take my life or take me out of this shitu*ation*. Year after year, I would beg for a release. The more

I prayed, the more challenging I felt that things would become.

Finally, after seven years of heartache and pain, the fights, the frustrations, the demands he placed on me, the requests to ignore Zaria and cater to him, the threats of him trying to shut my business down when he became angry, the alimony and spousal support case that he filed against me, the false police report he initiated against me as his backup plan to destroy my business, the sleepless and sexless nights, the gun threats, the loneliness, the emptiness, the mother-in-law, the monies he took from me out of my bank account, I WAS DONE!

Something in me said that my time with him was over. I needed GOD, and I needed him immediately. And then, IT WAS DONE. IT WAS OVER, and I WAS OUT!

For my child's safety and my sanity, I got out. I grappled with the thought that I was leaving this man while he was extremely ill. But I had done all that I could do for him for seven years. Besides, there was not anything in me that was telling me to stay.

In fact, everything in me said, run for your life. So, I ran. In fact, I ran like hell and didn't look back. I was too depleted and depressed to look back. I admit, I struggled with guilt for a long time because I felt like he really needed me. Yet, I left, and I chose to live with the guilt than die from the pain.

Finally, I demanded help. I demanded that his mom get involved in helping to care for her son. It was literally like pulling teeth trying to get his family members to move in and care for him. Even though I fled, I continued to pay for his bills and expenses for his care. I made certain to stay in communication with him, and I would even visit him to spend time with him on weekends. But I had to get out.

Coming out of that shit*uation* was daunting, and it was hard work. I stayed so long because I felt obligated to be there for him. For me, my vows were sacred, and I believed that I was sentenced to that environment for the life of the marriage. I convinced myself that the turmoil he caused my daughter and me was contractual and cemented in our holy matrimony. I was wrong. There was nothing Godly about this marriage from the beginning.

Those seven years of marriage brought me tremendous pain. During this time, I was isolated from everyone that I loved, and I was so lonely. I was so broken, depressed and extremely shamed because I had allowed myself to get ahead of GOD, and I had gotten myself into a shit*uation*. I had convinced myself that everyone that knew me and knew of our situation was laughing at me. I believed they were laughing because I had married this man I hadn't known for a very long time and soon after we met, we got married. I was convinced they laughed because everyone knew that I instantly went from being a new bride to his healthcare worker. And I felt that they were laughing at the fact that the man I loved had not only tried to destroy me emotionally but financially as well.

Still, I rise. I Leveled Up through this ordeal by making tough decisions and making a great deal of sacrifice and commitment. I forgave him for everything he had put me through, and then I forgave myself for leaving. You see, what I learned about forgiveness is this thing called GRACE and MERCY. I showed him grace for the hurt he caused me, and I begged GOD to have mercy on me for the decisions that I made and for the hurt that I might have caused him.

For some scary and unhealthy reason, I had insurmountable guilt about abandoning him while he was ill. I believed the toxic lie that being married meant staying in an emotionally, mentally and verbally abusive relationship was what I was supposed to do. It was a lie from the pit of hell, and I was done. Having an illness, addiction, or pain does not allow and authorize you to harass and inflict grief upon people. Suffering is not your right of passage for mistreating anyone. So, I got this revelation, and for once, I chose me. That day I decided that I had to go, and I had to let that guilt go!

Yes, that experience was excruciating but let me encourage you. Through harsh environments like this one or other shit*uations* that you are in, Leveling Up is doable and attainable. Just as I did, you too can break free from the chains that had you blocked, broken and stuck. If you have been wondering when your life will change – I say NOW! If you have been worrying if things could be better, I am screaming, HECK YEAH! If you have been praying and asking GOD for a sign, HERE IT IS!

Girlfriend, the choice is yours!!!!! You can keep the same things and remain in the same shit*uations*. Or you can put on your big girl panties and let's do this!

If you have never been through anything or if you feel as if you're all good, then this is not for you. Thank you for purchasing my book.

THE END.

On the other hand, if you are like the rest of us women who have had painful pasts, are facing challenges in your present and are looking for solutions to overcome obstacles in your future, pretty lady, you keep going because you are about to be FREE! Let's all take a break right here to use the ladies' room, pour yourself a glass of wine, grab your favorite pen and EXHALE! It's time to Level Up....

IT'S TIME TO LEVEL UP!

"This Level Up is about YOU and only YOU! It is less about impressing and more about improving! Stop seeking to impress others and start improving who you are and the way you do things, and they will automatically become impressed. "

April D. Graham

COMING OUT OF THE SHIT*UATION*

6 YOU ARE LOOSED TO LEVEL UP

As you read through these pages, you will soon discover that Sh%t Happens! Not just for me, not just for you, but for every living and breathing human being on this planet. No one is exempt from problems, so I need you to first let this sink in. However, some of us have experienced more trials and tribulations than you have the fingers to count. So, if that is you, you get a little more time to wallow in your sorrows a little longer (to the end of this page).

The Level Up is a REAL thing and not just a song by Ciara. Ladies, this is an actual and factual process of going from your good to your great. It is about taking a holistic and strategic approach to getting your sh%t together. YOU, as a whole woman, must commit to this process. The art of Leveling Up will require you to Identify your sh%t, Deal with your sh%t, Own your sh%t, Get out of your sh%t, Get into some sh%t, and be Confident in your sh%t.

As Ciara put it in her song Level Up,

I just keep elevating, no losses, just upgrading
My lessons, made blessings, I turned that into money
Thank God I never settled, this view is so much better
I'm chilling, I'm winning, like on another level

The Level Up process begins with answering these questions:

➢ Am I currently in any unhealthy situations? Identify them.

_____

➢ How do I spend most of my time?

_____

➢ What sort of people am I surrounded by? Positive or Negative?

_____

➢ What is my environment like? Is it clean, calm or chaotic, cluttered, and confusing?

_____

➢ How do I feel about myself? Am I happy, sad, blessed or depressed?

_____

➢ What things do I spend most of my time thinking about?

_____

➢ If I could change things, what would be different?

_____

REFLECTIONS, NOTES, IDEAS

There is one thing that GOD says to every believer regardless of their circumstance,

"TRUST ME"

Author Unknown

7 LOOK UP TO LEVEL UP

I must pause here (praise dance moment) because I cannot go any further without giving my Higher Power, (I call him ALMIGHTY GOD) HIS praise! Everything that I am, everything that I have, and everything I have come through, I attribute it to my faith. That's right, my faith in GOD!

The LOOK UP for me is the most important aspect of getting unstuck. Looking Up to a higher power, to be exact. If you are not a believer, you do not have anything to guide you, carry you, or cover you in challenging times. Let me be clear, I am not talking about religion. What I am referencing is something bigger! Something unimaginable! Something greater than you could have ever perceived. I am talking about a relationship.

Yes, the LOOK UP is about your relationship with GOD.

You are making a conscious effort to fortify your faith and trust into something bigger than what you can imagine. A surrendering of your soul to a force, idea, or concept that you recognize as GOD. It's a total dependence on what you heard and what you believe but can't touch or could hardly describe. It is relying on what Christians call the Holy Spirit to give you guidance and wisdom, and it is trusting HIM when you can't trace HIM.

Yes, I came out of my shit*uation* by looking up to GOD and by cultivating a relationship with HIM.

I would rise out of bed sometimes at 3 am and just sit on my floor in my closet, and I would weep and pray. I would study bible scriptures on healing, blessings, deliverance, faith, overcoming and trusting in the Lord. I would play worship music and sing songs of praise for hours.

This is your WHY! Not so much as why you are in the shit*uation*, but why it is crucial that you have a dependency on a higher power so that you can come out of it! In fact, looking up has little to do with you and everything to do with what you believe about your faith.

I can recall several occasions where I have been stuck and felt as if I did not have anywhere to run or anyone to run to. I was alone. I was afraid. I felt neglected by the people who were supposed to care and rejected by everyone and everything I thought I could depend on. Thankfully, I had my faith. My sure thing, my go-to for everything. It was just ME and MY GOD!

One incident specifically that I can recall was a situation that involved an accusation brought up against me. Actually, it wasn't an accusation; it was a blatant lie told against me.

In my young adult years, a young lady and I got into an argument over a situation involving my then-boyfriend. This argument became heated but never got physical. Let's call her "that girl" because I'm a Christian, and I don't want to use bit%h. She called the police and falsified a report stating that I physically attacked her and her children. I ended up getting arrested, transported to the county jail and charged with 2 misdemeanors and 4 felonies.

The next day, the judge released me on my own recognizance (ROR) to go home (google ROR, and you will see that When a criminal suspect is arrested, booked and granted release on their "own recognizance," or "R.O.R.," no bail money is paid to the court, and no bond is posted. The suspect is merely released after promising, in writing, to appear in court for all upcoming proceedings) PRAISE DANCE moment!!!!!!!

Who but a child of the Almighty God has this many charges and is released with no bond, and no house arrest, to just go home by signing their name and promising to appear in court. Let me say that again, I was charged with multiple felonies, and I was released the next day to go home on my own, with no bond, no house arrest…

TO GOD BE THE GLORY! But I still ended up having to fight this charge through the courts. Going through that process of getting to the truth was brutal. Although I knew I had not done what she accused me of, I was a young mother that believed that I could really go to jail and my kid be taken away from me. I was terrified. "Looking Up" in this shit*uation* was the only peace that I had. It was my only assurance that everything would be okay.

Eventually, I was acquitted of all charges, and she was actually charged for lying and falsifying a police report. Nonetheless, the remnants from this lie resurrected later on in my life.

I became an elementary school teacher, and the School District flagged me for re-fingerprinting. Although my record was sealed and expunged, the District had access to the arrest record. I was called downtown and was told that I was being terminated as a teacher because of this arrest. I needed an Attorney, and I needed one fast.

Though I couldn't afford one. I was young, newly married and struggling financially. My husband, ex #1, and I did not have any money or any other family members we could go to for help.

The Holy Spirit led me to reach out to my estranged Father. Let me say this was not easy. My dad did not play!!!! He was mean, hot-headed and quick-tempered. He carried several firearms and had no problem using any one of them at any given time.

Regardless, I was left with no other choice but to go to him. I mustered up the courage and went to my dad and asked him for the money to hire an attorney. Without any hesitation or any reservation, my dad gave me a signed blank check and sent me on my way to go and find an attorney.

Excuse me while I wipe my tears; this is another PRAISE BREAK moment for me. Did you get what I said? My mean and crazy dad, who I had been estranged from, gave me a blank check to go and hire an attorney. All I can say is that it could have only been GOD that orchestrated that.

This thing jeopardized my career, it compromised my family's livelihood, and it took a toll on me emotionally and financially. Thankfully, my Father in Heaven touched the heart of my father on earth, and he helped me.

Yes, I can hear some of you saying, but I always pray, and nothing happens like this for me. The reality is a lot happens when you pray, but the action takes place when you make a move.

Bible readers know the scripture – Faith without work is dead (James 2:14-26). I consider myself as someone who has great faith, but I had to do my work, and doing the work starts with

"Looking Up" to GOD for guidance, wisdom and support. This is a good place to meditate on Proverbs 3:5-6, "trust in the Lord with all of your heart and lean not unto your own understanding. In all of your ways, acknowledge HIM and HE shall direct your path."

Looking Up to God will inevitably level you up. This is you surrendering to your higher power by trusting him but also by activating your faith. It is making the necessary moves. It means making sacrifices, it's making adjustments, and making tough decisions. It's an awakening that happens in you that affirms that you can proceed with caution and confirms in you that the spirit is with you, so move forward in faith.

Trusting in GOD, higher power, etc., is probably the only guarantee that things will work out in your favor. It is your faith that will bring you through. So, let me remind you, letting go and Looking Up is the leverage you have when it is you against what you are facing.

"People can be at their most vulnerable, but still tenacious at the same time."

Toni Bernhard

8 LEVEL UP AND LEAD

To lead in a shit*uation* sometimes feels impossible. But, ladies, you can do it. All you need to do is LEAD:

L – Lean In

E - Eliminate

A - Adversity

D – Distractions

To LEAD simply means to Lean In and Eliminate Adversity and Distractions. It's taking authority over that thing that has created something so terrible that it has you immersed in this book—the thing that has you broken, blocked and stuck. No matter if you've been abandoned, abused, neglected, or rejected, etc., you can LEAD in any SHIT*UATION*!

The LEAD is you leaning into your purpose and doing everything you can to eliminate adversities and distractions to your destiny. Also, it is about refusing to be constantly reminded that it's what got you here in the first place. It is choosing to denounce that thing and no longer will you continue to be plagued by it.

The lead is getting the courage to say, I hear the whispers, and I constantly have the voices in my head as a daily reminder of my pain. However, it's done! It's over, and I won't be dealing with this crap ever again.

It is inevitable that you LEAD if you are going to Level Up. It is a strategy for taking authority over all the enemies that brought you the distress and sorrow in the first place. Sit with this for a minute because I need to highlight something here. If you are anything like me, you keep asking yourself, how is it that I keep getting into these situations? What is it about me that I keep falling into the same patterns? What do I lack to the point where my shortcomings overwhelmingly cost me and often sends me into the same struggles?

Journaling and getting to know yourself better can help you to answer this question. I recommend getting mine because it's inspirational, practical, and not to mention, it's beautiful. Write down some of the toughest situations you have been in and ask yourself – WHO WAS THERE? WHAT HAPPENED? WHY DID IT HAPPEN? WHERE DID IT HAPPEN? And HOW DID IT HAPPEN?

As I mentioned before, Leveling Up requires you to do your work, and part of your work is uncovering some truths about YOU!

Nonetheless, shift your perspective and lead in a way where you don't wait on a path to be created for you, but you create your own path by becoming the landscaper of your own life and trimming the hedges, plucking the weeds, and mowing down the grass to your distractions. We are no longer waiting for sh%t to happen but making sh%t happen. It is time to make it so that you MATTER!

Lead in your home by creating a space where everyone recognizes that you are the woman and warrior up in there, and everyone and everything must recognize that! You set the tone, you shift the atmosphere, and you control the flow of energy that flows through there.

It is about establishing a climate in your work/home environment by being intentional about having peace. When I enter your house, I do not care if you reside in an efficiency or a mansion; I should see, feel, and experience a home that says a woman lives here who is whole, in control, and this is a place where she is LEADING!

"And one day, she discovered that she was fierce, and strong, and full of fire, and not even she could hold herself back because her passion burned brighter than her fears."

Mark Anthony

9 LOOK FIERCE WHILE LEVELING UP

Are you one of those women who, when going through something, actually look like what you are going through? Clothes are always disheveled, hair is a mess, no make-up—you get my drift? If this is you, STOP IT RIGHT NOW and pull yourself together. Listen, I understand pain because I have dealt with it on so many different levels.

I have experienced heartbreak in so many areas of my life, and I know all too well how it feels to be hurt. I get it, that thing hurts down to your core that you can barely pull yourself up from the bed. Yes, it is devastating, but you must GET UP and SHOW UP!

I am not asking you not to feel what you feel. I am not looking for you to rid yourself of the emotions the shit*uation* caused. That sh%t hurt. That pain is real, and those emotions are raw. So, you are allowed to cry (and you should), you are allowed to be upset (and pissed off), but what I can't stand by and watch you do is dive into a den of despair each and every day.

There is an expiration date on sadness. And like everything else that expires, you will either need to throw it out or bury it. Eventually, you must come to the realization that each and every woman on this earth will have to walk through their own fiery furnace.

When I walked through my furnace, I had no one. It was me and me alone. So, I poured myself into ME. Although I did not get a lot of sleep during my toughest times, I would be intentional about rising out of bed an hour earlier to meditate and exercise. I would keep my hair done and dress up and present myself to the world as if I were okay.

You see, there's a new freedom that's called FIERCENESS. It is a mindset, an inner confidence that radiates even if you are hurting. I had to be intentional about walking in the "spirit" of FIERCENESS. I had to learn to lean into the evidence of the times I felt my most Beyonce self. The truth is, I was hurting.

Nonetheless, I convinced myself that if I looked good, I would feel better. It worked, for the most part. I felt that I could not allow my appearance to add to my list of problems. So, the days I felt that I was looking haute, those were the days I was feeling fierce, and those days seem a little easier than most.

I was working with a client who was going through difficult times and had totally neglected her appearance. She did not care anymore about what she looked like, and it showed. She was going through a divorce and was not coping well. Her entire being was wrapped up and trapped up in her relationship.

In her focusing solely on him, she neglected her. She abandoned everything else—her kids, her home, and herself. I am talking about not doing her hair, shaping her brows, waxing or so much as ironing her clothes when she left the house. This was totally unacceptable and definitely an added pressure that contributed to a deeper mental and emotional rut.

Through coaching this woman and many other women, I have learned that most of us are stressed and depressed, and it has nothing to do with US. In fact, it is the pain that others have afflicted upon us or the poison from others that we have poured into our own pores. So, the greatest challenge for getting free and becoming fierce is overcoming OTHER PEOPLE! What others think, what others say and how others feel keeps so many women from looking FIERCE.

So, beautiful woman, it's time to Level Up in your confidence and be fierce! Therefore, I come to declare your freedom today. I want you to get in front of a mirror and repeat these words. "No matter what happened in my life, I AM FREE! Each day I wake, I AM FREE. NO MATTER WHAT IS GOING ON AROUND ME, I AM FREE. No matter what size I am, I AM FREE. No matter what shape, color, height, or any other physical character or mental barrier we battle daily, I AM FREE."

Beautiful lady, you are FREE to be FIERCE!!!! Leveling Up in what you look like must be paramount when you are in a shit*uation*. I am not saying that you must become supermodel thin (Lord knows I have never been); I am talking about meeting your inner Sasha Fierce right where you are.

Looking fierce starts right at the very moment you decide to be free. Free from your shit*uation*, free from your insecurities, free from other people's judgments, opinions and free from your need to prove to others that you are great. The fact is you don't need to prove anything to anyone, just do YOU and others will take notice.

Fierceness is definitely mindset work. It is a state of mind and a faith walk that says, "I don't have to look like what I'm going through."

Ladies, get this in your spirit! Looking fierce has nothing to do with what you are going through, but everything to do with the woman you are and the woman you are becoming.

So, it is inevitable, when you allow yourself to wallow in a pool of sorrow, not only does your mental stability suffer, but your physical appearance will decline as well. When you are going through trials, that is not the time to become slack in your physical appearance. Get up, Dress up and Show up until you come through that shit*uation*.

REFLECTIONS

(What resonates with you up to this point?)

DISTRACTIONS

(What distracts you or keeps you stuck?)

NOTES & IDEAS

"Your mindset can take you places your money can't afford."

April D. Graham

Ladies, it's time to Level Up!
Are you ready for your
LEVOLUTION!

10 THE LEVOLUTION

The Levolution (the act of leveling up and evolving) is about getting free from the things that keep you from getting to your next level. If you are ready to get out of your shit*uation*, then you must be prepared for changes. This will be uncomfortable for many reasons, but mainly because it will require you to make tough decisions. Everything you know and all you are doing must be sifted and shifted towards your "coming out." This will begin with a shift in your mindset.

When I googled Mindset, it identified mindset as:

a mental inclination or disposition, or a frame of mind. Your mindset is your collection of thoughts and beliefs that shape your thought habits. And your thought habits affect how you think, what you feel, and what you do.... beliefs. Basically, mindset is how you see yourself, is what you will become.

This is powerful because not only will your mindset affect you and what you do, this could potentially be a determining factor for not only how you live and navigate life, but your kids and grandkids too.

So often, this hidden treasure called mindset is overlooked. When things happen to us, depending on your mindset, in the ashes, you will rise, or you will choose to remain in the fire and be burned up.

Let us look at some burning shitua*tions* that have kept most women stuck.

Raise a hand if you have been:

- Molested
- Neglected
- Abandoned
- Rejected
- Used
- Abused
- Divorced
- Divorced again
- Insecure
- Ignored
- Ashamed
- Talked about
- Cheated on

- Lied on
- Mistreated
- Taken advantaged of
- Overlooked
- Underpaid
- Broken
- Alone
- Afraid

I can raise a hand for every item on this page, and if you can identify with ALL or SOME of these items, it is time for your LEVOLUTION!

YOU ARE IN A SHITUATION, but YOU ARE ABOUT TO COME OUT!

And this is how you will do it!

"You may not control all the events that happen to you, but you can decide not to be reduced by them."

Maya Angelou

11 LEVEL UP – IDENTIFY YOUR SH%T

STEP 1

Stop Acting As Though You Do Not Know What It Is

CALL A THING A THING is what I heard Iyanla Vanzant screaming at a guest on her television show. This statement resonated with me because I believe that Iyanla was screaming, "it is what it is," - so stop dismissing it, stop denying it, and stop acting as though it did not happen. In essence, what she was saying is, it's time to become vulnerable and put a name to it.

Identifying your Shit*uation* is just that. Identify it, put a name to it and call a thing a thing! There is no chance of getting out of something that has you stuck if you do not clearly understand what that something is.

This will be a "get real" moment for you (as I told you before, "put your big girl panties on and handle this")! It will probably hurt like heck, and most likely, you will experience certain feelings with identifying the shit*uation*, but this is necessary. As I once heard someone say, you cannot conquer what you won't confront.

__INSERT NAME__

you are going to have to come to terms with some ugly truths. Truths such as why do I have this problem? Did I cause this problem? Or am I the problem? You must ask questions like, what is it within me that has allowed this shit*uation*, accepted this shit*uation* or keep attracting these shit*uations* to the point that it has become the norm.

It is imperative that you get honest with yourself. Become vulnerable (no judgment here) until you have reached that moment of clarity to shout: I AM IN THIS MESS, but I AM COMING OUT!!

LET ME BE CLEAR
__(name it)__

Is the shit*uation* that I am coming out of!

Hopefully, you have identified the situation, but if you're anything like me, you tend to overthink things. Therefore, let me help you to identify your Shit*uation*! Answer the following questions:

- What keeps me up at night?
- Who or what is causing me pain?
- Who or what constantly keeps me upset?
- Why does this person/thing make me feel this way?
- Who or what has mentally drained me?
- If I can change ONE situation, what would it be?
- What are your struggles?
- Do you feel stuck in a situation?
- When was the last time you experienced joy?
- What would peace look like to you?

Identifying your shit*uation* is probably the most imperative step to getting out of the shit*uation* because if you don't acknowledge it, you will continue to ignore it as though it doesn't exist.

After you have identified your sh%t, you are now ready to OWN YOUR Sh%t!

"At the end of the day we are accountable to ourselves - our success is a result of what we do."

CATHERINE PULSIFER

12 LEVEL UP – OWN YOUR SH%T

STEP 2

The act of taking accountability!

The second step is Owning your Shit*uation* by being accountable. So many people are stuck because they have not owned their sh%t. You have yet to be accountable for your part in the situation. Not owning your sh%t is a very dangerous posture because, in this space, you remain the victim. Either you have disconnected from reality, refused to confront it or you continue to blame the other party for the hurt you have experienced from the situation.

Here's the thing, every circumstance that has happened, every breakdown in the relationship that has occurred, and every hardship that you've experienced – you have a part it in!

Meaning, you may not have caused the Shit*uation*, but you are accountable for how you react, recover, and respond.

One of my own personal Shit*uations* was being angry with my mom for many years. My mom was a self-professed addict that would often neglect us, leaving us in the hand of an abuser.

My siblings and I practically raised ourselves because of her addiction. HER negligence caused ME years and years of feelings of insecurity, abandonment, isolation, rejection, neglect, and a defeated mindset. I was very bitter because of my childhood and held on to this anger towards her for so many years.

The relationship was strained, and it was challenging trying to develop a mother/daughter bond, and I blamed her for it. I was so mad with her, and I struggled with forgiving her for being addicted to drugs and alcohol.

I would have anxiety on Mother's Day because it was challenging for me to pick out a Mother's Day card. I would literally be in the discount store forever trying to find the right card with the right words to say. I felt that the words that I wanted to say to my mom were not represented in any of the cards.

All the Mother's Day cards would read: you raised me to be a strong woman, you have given me the best life, I have always loved you, I look up to you, mom, etc. You see, I wanted my card to say:

Dear Mom,

I know you told me you did the best you knew how to do, but that was not good enough to take the pain away. I needed to hear you say that you are sorry and that you wish that you could take the pain and terrible memories away. I struggle with issues of being alone because I am afraid that I will have things to happen to me or get hurt or violated again. I wish you would have tried harder to get off drugs and to build a better relationship, but it seems that you chose not to deal with what happened in our past. However, what I want to say is that I love you, and I have forgiven you, and I'm so thankful that the shortcomings that you had with your kids, you made up for it and are a loving grandma to your grandkids. Also, mom, I am not too old to hear I love you, I'm proud of you and

I support you!

As a young adult, I decided to start my healing process, and I decided to confront her. I sought this option anticipating a much needed, I am SORRY! To my surprise, she did not have one for me. She offered NO APOLOGY. She accepted NO RESPONSIBILITY, and last but not least, she took NO ACCOUNTABILITY!

Go figure! In fact, her response was, "I did the best I knew how to do" (still blown away by this answer to this very day). She insisted that, as an addict, her actions were beyond her control. Mom justified her absence and our painful childhood by blaming it on her addiction.

Mom shared that something traumatic happened to her in her past that perpetuated her drug and alcohol abuse. Don't get me wrong, I totally empathize and understand this, but it doesn't erase how she chose to cope and how the decisions she made affected her kids.

Ultimately, mom rejected the fact that she was accountable for healing from her past hurts and pains and raising her girls accordingly. Nevertheless, I forgave my mom (in fact, she lives with me). I forgave my mom because I realized that I am not accountable for the pain that was caused by her, but I am accountable for healing from it.

The people who have hurt you may never apologize or acknowledge your pain, or accept accountability, but that's okay. One of my favorite people (my baby sister) once told me to "be done with having expectations for how other people should act or respond." She said that we expect people to do what we want them to do, but they might not know how or be ready to do it.

Forgiving my mom was not easy, but it was necessary. It was necessary because as I continued to internalize that hurt, the effects of unforgiveness eventually became visible externally (irritability, tiredness, weight gain, skin problems, etc.).

It was also necessary to forgive because, as a Christian woman, I am required by GOD to forgive.

Yes, it's true; forgiveness is mandatory for Christians. If I'm honest, I struggled with this part because I could not understand why GOD would require me to forgive my dad, who neglected me, my mom, that rejected me, the abuser, the attacker and the pain inflictor for everything that they had done to me.

Well, GOD gave me the answer to why it was required of me, and it was straight to the point:

GOD says, I forgave YOU for the ones that You hurt, used, abused, rejected and neglected and I have required your victims to release and forgive YOU!

Wow, thinking about this revelation that GOD gave me still makes me cry like a baby. Our Heavenly Father wants us to hold ourselves accountable for the same things we require of others. Think about this, the things that we say and the things that we do bring pain and suffering to others as well. My sisters, if we are going to Level Up to be whole and complete Women of GOD, we must all take accountability for the things that we have done to hurt people and not hold ourselves to a different standard of accountability.

I admonish you today to hold yourself accountable and GET FREE! Today is a good day to repent for unforgiveness, ask for forgiveness from the people you have hurt, and forgive those who have hurt you and HEAL.

You are accountable to YOU! You are accountable for how YOU heal, and you are accountable for how YOU will move forward.

Be kind and compassionate to one another, forgiving each other, just as in Christ God forgave you.

<u>Ephesians 4:32</u>, NIV

Do not judge, and you will not be judged. Do not condemn, and you will not be condemned. Forgive, and you will be forgiven.

<u>Luke 6:37</u>, NIV

And when you stand praying, if you hold anything against anyone, forgive them, so that your Father in heaven may forgive you your sins.

<u>Mark 11:25</u>, NIV

"If I was meant to be controlled, I would have come with a remote!"

Author Unknown

13 LEVEL UP – DEAL WITH YOUR SH%T

STEP 3

Refusing to be controlled by people, things or circumstances that placed you in that sh#%

A client reached out to me to seek advice about her bad marriage. After learning that her husband leaves home every day, ALL day, doesn't help with the kids, is emotionally and verbally abusive and removes the tag from the car so that she is unable to drive, I still refrained from advising this woman to leave her husband!

The truth is, she already knows the answers to the questions that she was asking. Therefore, my response to her was two-fold:

- what is your inner voice speaking to you (your gut, holy spirit, internal alarm)?

(2) in this Shit*uation*, what are some of the things you are in control of (are your kids cared for, what can you do to work on yourself)?

After answering these questions, we identified the things that were controlling her and what was at the root of her Shit*uation*. One being her perspective. She was focused only on her problem and never took a solution-driven approach. Her entire conversation would be about what she lacked and what she lost. I encouraged her to shift her perspective on what she did have in her favor.

One being, her husband was away from the home majority of the day, leaving this space for her to grow. I would argue that this was a great opportunity for her to learn her identity and discover who she was as a person aside from her husband. Uncover some truths about her, learn her strengths and identify areas where she needed growth. She had this space to pray, meditate, take an online course, start a business, and plan strategically to get out of that mess.

Here's the thing, often when we get ourselves into problems, we sit in those problems wallowing and feeling sorry for ourselves. Yes, I as well, have stayed in my slump for longer than I should have. Yet, what I discovered in my journey to breaking free was that your pit is only supposed to be a PIT STOP! A place for you to feel pity, ponder, pray and then persevere. However, we let our problems become greater than our praise! During these times, we should get still before the Lord to hear his instructions and shift our focus from the foolery and focus on our faith by drawing nearer to HIM!

In case you are wondering what happened to the client, she took my advice and shifted her perspective. She started praising GOD for what she did have control of (her kids, health, food, shelter, a computer, etc.) and placed her energy into the things that served her growth. She would do in-home workouts, started online classes, and started a business.

She is doing amazing now…when her husband looked up, she was 20 pounds lighter, business was taking off and she had managed to save enough money to purchase her own car and eventually move out.

I would never advise any woman to leave her husband (unless it's physical abuse) because I, too, didn't leave until I had the courage to become uncontrolled!

Being uncontrollable means that you prayerfully and strategically implement a plan and create a process that will place you in control. In other words, let us be driven to identify the problems and commit to finding solutions.

I was in a pit from staying in a toxic marriage for over 15 years. I endured emotional and verbal abuse, I endured cheating, cold and distant behavior, the birth of a child with his mistress, lack of support, no intimacy, etc., for the sake of my kids. That was the BIGGEST mistake I have ever made.

You see, a broken, sad, and downtrodden mom was raising broken, sad and downtrodden kids! The emotional, financial, and "marital" control was breaking me down and crushing my children daily. The things ex #1 DID to me crushed me but the things he SAID to me, broke me down! His words were so harsh and hurtful they would control my entire mood for the entire day.

You see, I was able to move past the affairs and the child he had with his mistress. However, I could never get those harsh names out of my head. How in the heck did I allow HIS words to shape MY reality???

You know how? I had low self-esteem and lacked confidence, and I was broken. So, one day, I chose ME, and I was done with the countless days of depression and despair. I was hurt, but I was no longer going to be held back. I vowed to become uncontrollable.

There was no chance in hell that I would allow this man or that situation to continue to control me or cage me in out of fear, obscurity, or insecurities. Does that mean I packed up and left immediately? NO! I prayed, planned, got therapy, and sought wise counsel from my pastor and a spiritual leader, and then I strategically removed myself and my kids from that toxic environment.

No longer being controlled by your SHIT*uation* is to reverse or bring an end to the very thing that has you stuck. I believe that when we as women are devalued, it is because that is the lesson that we have been teaching others about ourselves and the message that we are allowing others to receive.

Somewhere in this toxic relationship, we have said (or have communicated by way of accepting this behavior) I am okay with this! So, whether it is a toxic relationship, a bad decision or a crisis that was no fault of our own, it is time to be done with being controlled by the Shit*uation*.

It is time to tell that thing that has been controlling you, I am not okay with this, and I vow to be uncontrollable!

> "Accept what is, let go of what was, and make changes towards what will be. Life's about taking action."
>
> Kristen Butler

NOTES & IDEAS

14 LEVEL UP – GET OUT OF YOUR SH%T

STEP 4

The art of taking action

Step 3 of getting out of your Shit*uation* requires something big – wait for it, are you ready? Here it is. A SHIFT IN YOUR MINDSET! Yes, it is that big yet, that simple! Being actionable is a big step because it requires a shifting of your mindset from victim to victorious. It is when you make the decision to see yourself differently, view your situation differently, and approach things differently.

Your outlook becomes brighter, and your perspective is clear. Your words and thoughts are no longer that you cannot believe that this has happened. You now say things like, it happened, and I cannot change it, and I will learn and grow from this.

I can attest to the fact that if you change your mindset, you can change your life. I was in a Shit*uation* where I was passed over for a promotion. My immediate boss was moved into another position, and I was basically already doing this job of that administrative position. Needless to say, the position was not given to me but to someone that had alliances and connections that I couldn't compete with. Naturally, I became angry, pissed off, and bitter.

In my heart, I knew that I deserved that promotion. I knew the job. I did the work. I put in the time and commitment. I earned the right to that promotion! Well, apparently, the higher-ups didn't think so. I was devastated, I felt rejected (AGAIN), and I was humiliated because I was training others for this position, and I was embarrassed because my colleagues were all being promoted.

I realized that this situation was breaking me down mentally, so I shifted my mindset. I could not allow things beyond my control to keep me stuck. I started dreaming about the life I wanted and began creating the new life I envisioned. My mindset became, I will become my own boss and will not allow this to happen to me again. No one will have the authority to tell me what to do or not appreciate what I had to offer. So, I took action and opened my own preschool. Get this, it will take several of those positions to earn what I earn from taking this leap.

This step is really the hub of where "getting your Shit*uation* together resides. Ladies, hear me clearly, the mindset shift is the most critical action step, and it will take a lot of intentional effort on your part. As the cliché goes, whether you think you can or can't, you're right. It's all in the mindset!

Nonetheless, with the appropriate action steps (established and executed), your life will change. I can assure you that if you are stuck in a Shit*uation*, a shift in your mindset is mandatory for breaking through. If you have a problem, change your mindset, and find a solution. If you are your problem, change your mindset and be the solution.

NOTES & IDEAS

> *"I'm unavailable most of the time because my time is being invested in my growth. I'm leveling up, focusing on my own sh%t, and I've got work to do."*
>
> *Kylie Francis*

15 LEVEL UP – GET INTO YOUR SH%T

STEP 5

You must avoid any and everything that is a distraction to your goals

Get into your sh%t means making yourself unavailable to any and everything. This is going to be a must for getting out of your SHIT*uation*! This is a prerequisite for living a happier and more fulfilled life. Let me explain. Becoming unavailable does not mean that you fly off to a foreign country alone or sever ties to the real-world. However, to be unavailable will require a level of disconnection from all things toxic that has been the driving force in your SHIT*uation*.

Toxic things, toxic people, and toxic places – all have to go!

If it does not produce good fruit, it is toxic. In fact, the Bible puts it this way *–you will know them by their fruit*. This principle can be applied in every area of your life. You can look over every situation you are in and ask yourself, is there any "good fruit"?

Survey your relationship, friends, job, etc., to see if there is good fruit. In your relationship, if you and your mate have not set and established plans that will lead to a prosperous and productive relationship– it is toxic.

If you and your girlfriends are still gossiping and not goal-setting, it's toxic. If places you are visiting cause you to act and become less than the woman of GOD that you are, it's toxic! If you are showing up to work only to collect a paycheck, it's toxic. There should be consistent evidence of growth personally and professionally. If you cannot identify any areas in your life that have produced "good fruit," it's time to remove yourself from that SHIT*uation because it's toxic!*

Nevertheless, the oxymoron is this – getting out of your SHIT*uation* is actually going to require you to get into it! In other words, by *getting out* of YOU and by *getting into* YOU! In this step, you must be unavailable to anything that is not positive and productive and has been keeping you stuck. Then, you will need to place your time and energy into YOU! Yes, it's going to be very challenging because everyone and everything up until this point has had free access to you.

In reality, they have paid nothing to harass your mind, control your emotions, and make deposits into your despair. The fact of the matter is, by staying stuck, you have discounted your destiny and provided coupons to your purpose!

Here's the thing, if you are still in bondage to some of the same SHIT*uations* year after year, the only way to break free is by making yourself unavailable to work on YOU! And I mean, to really work on you to show up as your best authentic self.

I was working with a young lady that seemingly had it all together. She was cute in the face and thin in the waist. I mean very attractive, wore the finest apparel, knew all of the fancy fine dining places, hot guys falling at her feet, had a career as a teacher within the public school system, but she is what I would call a "dressed up mess."

I say this because she was constantly at the center of the mess and stress. She attracted the guys, but they were of no substance, she competed with her girlfriends instead of collaborated with them, and she was always broke and borrowing money. I mean, a real hot mess!

Listen, ladies, you really have to get real with yourself if you are going to get out of your shit*uation*. You can't keep walking around looking like you have it all together when the truth is that you're broken, insecure, lack integrity, immature and have a heart full of malice. Stop it immediately and grow up and start doing the work to show up!

Leading Lady, get all the way into YOU and get yourself together! If money is your SHIT*uation*, stop spending and learn to save and budget! If credit is your problem, seek help and get credit counseling. If your bills are not paid, learn to balance your finances or start a side hustle. If you are stuck in a rut on the job, seek a promotion or elevate your skills and find a new job.

The good news is this – there is a way out of every

SHIT*uation (drops mic)*, but you make yourself unavailable to the very things that have imprisoned you thus far and use that time of disconnection to work on you!

"Successful people often exude confidence – it's obvious that they believe in themselves and what they're doing. It isn't their success that makes them confident, however. The confidence was there first."

Travis Bradberry

16 LEVEL UP – BE CONFIDENT IN YOUR SH%T

STEP 6

Become confident in knowing that you've WON before you even STARTED

There is no doubt that you will be afraid to move forward, but I've learned that fear limits you and your vision. It serves as blinders and cripples you from what is actually in store for you. Nonetheless, the good news is that once you make up your mind and change your mindset, nothing can stop you!

Ladies, I speak from experience because I, too, had to find confidence through the many life trials and struggles. Below is one *shituation* that really crushed my spirit and shook my confidence to the core.

I was a teacher for our local school district. I was respected by the students and my peers and was identified by my boss as one of the school leaders. He was really proud of the work that I was doing with the staff and students and encouraged me to become a School Administrator. For the first time in my life, someone believed in me.

Wow, what an amazing feeling that was, to be told that you MATTER! Nonetheless, not knowing my purpose and not having a plan, I was reluctant.

Thankfully, I grew confident in the work I was doing as a Teacher, and I followed his advice and pursued my degree in Educational Leadership. I worked hard, y'all, and I DID IT! I graduated with my Educational Specialist Degree in Educational Leadership.

The time had come, and I was finally ready to be promoted to Assistant Principal. It was a bittersweet feeling because I was loved by my current school family and was respected by my school leaders. Then, one day I am summoned to the Principal's office. Finally, I got the call from the Regional Director. I was told to report to the new school – "You are the new Assistant Principal." After the non-stop thank you Jesus, WOW, WOW, WOW was all I remember saying next.

I was overcome with excitement and overjoyed with gratitude. It was all because I had never seen that for myself. The day had come that I got what I had been praying for. I was an Assistant Principal, a school leader, and a key element in ensuring thousands of children's safety and success. My salary increased instantly by $30,000 annually. Not to mention, I was assigned up under the leadership of an African American female.

I was ecstatic because I felt that she would support and mentor me. Little did I know, that was so far from what actually happened. Can you believe what I thought would be an ideal situation turned out to be a horrible nightmare?

This black female boss gave me hell. She was rude, crude, and overall, not a good person. The staff referred to her as a bonafide micro-manager, whose claim to fame was "not taking any crap." This woman was so harsh and tough on me that the stress was literally making me physically ill. She contributed to a 50-pound weight gain, and I, a go-getter young woman, was broken in my career. She was nothing short of a dream stealer and destiny killer.

Yes, I know "dream stealer" and "destiny killer" are harsh words but let me explain. This woman made my life a living hell. Here I am, a NEW administrator, straight out of the classroom who obviously did the work to be there.

She didn't care, nor was she concerned that I was a novice in this new role and would assign tasks to me that most veteran admins struggled to complete.

Nonetheless, I didn't complain, and besides, I was always one up for a challenge. Then it was the public humiliation that she would spew out if something was not done to her satisfaction. Like, the day I forgot to put the palm trees on the stage for the Honor Roll Assembly. She walked to the microphone and said, "sorry for not having the palms trees here to make the stage beautiful; I gave the job to an empty wagon."

Even that didn't break me. It was the countless unplanned, unscheduled administrator meetings that she would schedule thirty minutes prior to me going home that nearly broke me down.

My baby was a student in this school, and this woman knew that. My child would be crying and screaming that she was starving while I would be forced to wait on her to commence the meeting. She would schedule the meeting at 4:30 but wouldn't call me in to meet until 6pm. Not to mention, I had an hour commute home. She would spend countless hours in that school and expected me to do the same.

From the moment I opened my eyes in the morning (she would call me at 6 am, and I didn't have to report until 8 am) until the time I would leave that building, this woman would degrade me, criticize me and complain about what needed to have been done.

I would cry every day and live off of fast food because this woman was so demanding. I was gaining weight so rapidly that I hardly noticed myself in the mirror. I felt like I was nearing a break down from the stress, and I knew that I could not continue in that way.

So, I started speaking up and placing boundaries. No longer would I answer the 6 am calls or stay for the unscheduled three-hour meetings. For sure, you know that didn't go well with her. You guessed right if you guessed that she retaliated!

This Principal (black female boss) who I thought would mentor, support, and develop me (an up and coming black female administrator) retaliated. She changed my work assignment, ignored me, was harsh with me, and did not acknowledge me as one of the school leaders, and on top of that, she gave me an unsatisfactory evaluation.

I was in shitu*ation* at work, and I needed out. Needless to say, my way out came. I refused to sign the unfavorable evaluation, so she asked that I be reassigned from her school. The Regional Director had heard great things from my former Principal, and so he was willing to give me another chance to demonstrate the talent that he knew I possessed.

He reassigned me to another school with a Hispanic woman as the Principal. The day I reported to my new school, she called me in her office and says, "you don't come highly recommended from your last Principal, but you have a clean slate with me." She basically told me her expectations and then released me to do my job.

Before I walked out of her office, the last thing she said was, "If I have to do it, then I don't need you." I remember thinking to myself, you are not going to have to do sh%t! You will see! I will prove that heffa wrong! I am going to do this job like no other Assistant Principal in this District, and I won't be stopped.

As a school Assistant Principal, you have the worst job in the District, there is no union to support you, and horrible Principals use this as leverage to hold you hostage to their demands. I refused to let that be a crutch for me. I changed my mindset from discouraged to one of determined. I was confident that I knew my stuff and that I was good at the job and only needed support and guidance. I needed a chance, and I knew that this was my opportunity to get that chance. So, heck yes, I was going after it!

I had to Level Up to prove something to the destiny killer,

my Regional Director, my new boss, and most importantly, to myself. I leveled up by reaching out to other Assistant Principals from other school districts. I wanted to introduce my current staff to something new and innovative. I leveled up by embracing the change and forming leadership clusters that served as my agents of change.

Ultimately, I leveled up by mastering something that this school staff knew nothing about, Data-Driven instruction.

I introduced this new teaching concept as an instructional learning tool that galvanized learning. I established their trust and built relationships that ended up changing the educational landscape of the school.

In the final analysis, we excelled. We became a high-performing school, and I was a major component in making that happen. So much so that only after two years in this school and I was promoted. I was promoted to one of the most coveted positions as an Assistant Principal. I was appointed to open a newly built, state-of-the-art Middle School.

Me, with no connections, no alignments and with a salty, shady, yet splendid leadership track record. I made history. I was the first Assistant Principal of this school. Therefore, it is imperative to find your confidence when you have goals and dreams! On your journey, you must be certain in the things that you believe you were created for.

Here's the thing, any and everything will try and deter you from going after the things that GOD has placed in your heart.

What I thought would be my ideal situation turned out to be my worst job ever throughout my twenty-year tenure with the District.

The destiny killer and dream stealer did everything in her power to break me. Truth be told, she hurt me to my soul and made me question my very essence as a school leader. That experience shook me to my core. I wanted to give up. I wanted to change careers, and I wanted to stop.

Like the other women in my life who I thought would support and protect me, this woman was another reminder of the voices that said I wasn't good enough, smart enough or capable enough. She broke my spirit in more ways than I care to discuss. However, I had enough confidence to know that I belonged in Leadership, and I was determined to prove her wrong.

"She was unstoppable not because she did not have failures or doubts, but because she continued on despite them!"

Beau Taplin

17 LEVEL UP – BE UNSTOPPABLE IN YOUR SH%T

STEP 7

Become unstoppable in becoming the woman that GOD created you to be

Soledad O'Brien (broadcaster and executive producer) once said, "the journey must be unstoppable if the joy is going to be undeniable. Leading Lady, you were meant to live an abundant life (don't take my word, read John 10:10), overflowing with blessings. Why settle for anything less than that which has been promised to you?

The distractions and destiny killers will always be present, but I learned to not allow disappointments and fear to paralyze me and make me lose focus. Ladies, if you are going to get to your next level, it's imperative that you do the same.

I know you've been stuck, and I know you're afraid, but I also know that you can't let it stop you from trying new things. If you have been waiting for permission to be great – here it is! You now have GOD's approval and my permission to become the *best* version of yourself.

Being *unstoppable* is just that! It is refusing to allow anyone or anything to stop you from coming out of the SHIT*uation*. You must sidestep distractions and dismiss disappointments that attempt to derail you from your plan. There will always be something that will serve as a barrier to your breakthrough, but you must have the faith and fearlessness to overcome it.

Onward and Upward must be at the core of who you are becoming. Yes, you will be afraid. Of course, you are going to make a mistake. News flash, the slip is inevitable. Still, your mindset must be – I have an action plan, and I plan on working it (snaps finger)!

Believe in yourself. Do what you love.

Become **UNSTOPPABLE!!!**

(_____**insert name**_____)

the world is waiting on you!

Leveling Up is not easy. If it was, every one of us would be operating at our fullest potential, and we are not. The reality is most of us are only surviving at best. We have conditioned ourselves to accept "I am ok." I wanted more than that. I was not comfortable with "OK." I needed more. In fact, I craved more and yearned for different. I wanted to find out just what would happen if I actually stepped out on faith and trusted GOD.

I needed to know that this drive and determination that was inside of me was not for naught. You see, I had a different kind of hunger. I had soul starvation. There were days that I even wondered why I ever existed. Well, the answer to that was, because of YOU! GOD needed me to let you know that there are levels to this thing called life. It will not always be easy, and the path will not always be smooth, but it's doable, you're capable, and it's possible to have the things you pray for.

Every person on the planet has and will need to Level Up at some point in their life. So, The Levolution was written as a solution for doing just that. By changing the mindset and believing that you can. By going on your own personal mission to accomplish your goals and seeing this as a movement for the rest of your life to -Level Up. Some days I still struggle. Most days, I must still affirm my worth. Again, no days will I ever stop going after everything that I work and pray for.

To level up, I needed to put in the work and effort. So, I learned to be disciplined. My mindset was wake, pray, and slay. In that order, I still approach each day. I challenge ME, compare me with ME, and my only competition is MYSELF!

As women, we tend to lose focus and have taken our eyes off our priorities, our purpose, and the promises of GOD. You are so significant in this world, but you will not tap into that significance until you become unstoppable in your mission and vision.

> Sis, what are you waiting for? We need your gifts and talents. The world is waiting on you!

18 LEVEL UP – BE UNDENIED IN YOUR SH%T

STEP 8

Refuse to be denied of the things you work and pray for

There was not a chance in hell that I was going to be denied again. I mean, I have allowed so many people to have their way with me either emotionally, physically or mentally. This time around, I chose ME! I made up my mind to focus on the things that added value to my life and would shut down and shut out everything else that was contrary to that.

I started by deprogramming my mind and undoing the negative words spoken to me and over me. As my Bishop puts it – rewrite the narrative and nullify the prediction that was spoken over you! I literally took these words to heart. I kept asking myself, how did I let the words of others shape who I was and who I was becoming? This had to stop!

I removed the words that ex #1 said to me *("you are a fat bit@h and only a Jamaican man is going to want your big a%%"),* and I replaced them with the words that GOD said to me (*you are the apple of my eye*).

Don't get me wrong, on my journey of being undeniable, there were definitely triggers and stressors along the way. The more they came, the more I leaned in and relied on my Heavenly Father to speak to me and give me direction.

GOD gave me this message one day:

Women have allowed so many men to woo them with their words but have not even given a second thought about GOD's words that HE has spoken to us. (Read that part again)! Think about how foolish we have been for a man because he said those sweet words to us (you're beautiful, you're my everything, I love you, etc.), and we would do just about anything for them, trust everything that they say, offer gifts and would give soooo freely to support them and their cause. Now think about what GOD says to us (you are fearfully and wonderfully made, you're royalty, you're the apple of his eye, you're precious, etc.), and we have done NOTHING for HIM. No witnessing, no serving others, no faith, no tithing, no sacrificial offerings, no fulfilling purpose.

Like the church says, if you can't say Amen, say ouch! This revelation blew my mind. The truth is those harsh words that man spoke contributed to our brokenness, and we believed man every time. Shamefully, all of the words that GOD has spoken, words that would bless and strengthen us, were not even given a second thought.

I also became undenied by becoming the CEO of my own life. I needed to recreate who I was as my own boss and then align myself with other leaders whose individual purpose was to elevate their personal brand. I was unapologetically passionate about pursuing my purpose. That included saying NO to people, removing some friends, and loving family members from a distance.

I moved quickly as I allowed GOD to redesign my life. I wasn't going to allow the inner critic to have her way with me again. I didn't hesitate or procrastinate with the things that GOD was leading me towards. I would pray (sometimes fast), listen and then move. And when GOD didn't unction me to move, I worked on my mind, body and spirit, but I worshipped in my waiting. Everything became about ME and GOD and then everyone else.

Another thing I did to become undeniable was learning from and not living in my past failures. One thing is for sure, the path to freedom and success is not linear. You've heard the stories of countless women having to overcome past mistakes and grow from them.

Here are a few that you might have heard of:

For decades, Martha Stewart was world famous for her brand of simple, elegant homemaking tips and home decor; her stamp of approval was worth billions. Then she was charged with insider trading and was sentenced to five months in prison, fined $195,000 and forced to step down from her company. Since released from prison, she has a TV show with Snoop Dogg and now her current net worth is estimated at $300 million.

Dorothy Hamill is a gold medalist in figure skating in the 1976 Winter Olympics. She used this fame and fortune and made millions by becoming a star in a number of professional ice-skating shows, a spokesperson for multiple companies, and endorsing products such as cars, coffee and shampoo. But Dorothy fell into bad financial habits by overspending on jewelry and making other decisions that forced her to file for bankruptcy. Since then, she's written a book, A Skating Life: My Story, starred in the television movie The Christmas Angel: A Story on Ice, and appeared in the 2007 movie Blades of Glory alongside Will Ferrell. Dorothy's net worth is now $5 million.

Oscar-winning actress Halle Berry is a perfect example of a person who, through hard work and the unwillingness to give up on her dreams, pulled herself from extreme poverty to unbelievable wealth. She moved to New York City with the hope of becoming an actress but soon ran out of money and had to live in a homeless shelter. She was 21-years-old at the time, and spent her days going to auditions and her nights at the shelter in the Big Apple. Her mother refused to give her money because she wanted Halle to become independent and learn the value of money on her own.

Then there are everyday people who we can look to for inspiration. One person, particularly for me, is my cousin, Andrea Hankerson. She was a teen mom who dropped out of high school. Andrea did the work on HER. She took chances by *enrolling in classes to earn her GED. She made changes by disconnecting from certain people and things that were unhealthy. She changed her mindset and made choices like to pursue her Bachelor's and Master's Degree. Andrea struggled with two failed marriages, toxic relationships and brokenness. Currently, she is happily married to the man she calls her "gift from GOD." She is an administrator in her day job and has a successful investment company. She owns multiple real estate projects alongside her husband.*

I could go on and on with stories of women who failed and how they overcame. On the other hand, why should I? If you need more to convince you to give GOD and YOU a chance to get unstuck, then you're not ready and you should seek out other support.

Like I said in the opening chapter of this book, getting unstuck is grown woman stuff. You have to be ready mentally and willing physically. Clearly, you can see the constant in each lady's story. We all experienced pain, but we were all undeniable in pursuing our goals and living in our passion. We stepped outside of our comfort zones, and we learned from our failures.

Lastly, I became undeniable by seeking out the promises of GOD in my life. I was relentless in pursuing my passion and discovering my purpose. I would meditate on scriptures related to purpose and the promises of GOD. I bought books, listened to CDs, watched Christian TV, attended church conferences, fast, prayed, and looked to spiritual leaders for confirmation. And then, I would fast and pray some more.

Yes, I know, this sounds like a lot. Bishop TD Jakes once said, "the good stuff costs." Ladies, living meagering is easy. It doesn't cost a thing, and it doesn't require you to do much. However, I choose to live an abundant life (John 10:10), and I wanted the "good stuff" in life and the good stuff costs.

I desired to be a vessel for the kingdom of GOD, and I stayed in GOD'S presence until HE revealed to me what that would look like for ME.

I had a vision of how I wanted to live and the things that I wanted to do while I was living. I chose to be prosperous and productive. I wanted to live an impactful life and not one of obscurity. With GOD's grace and guidance, I combined my faith with being fearless and became undeniable in the things that I believed GOD for and the life that I envisioned for myself.

NOTES & IDEAS

19 LEVEL UP – BE UNBREAKABLE IN YOUR SH%T

STEP 9

Stand firm in the face of your adversities

Yes, suffering from Brokenness and being stuck is a real thing. Nevertheless, what's also real is that your story is not over unless you choose to stay in that Shituation! Nothing you've gone through or nothing that you will ever face will disqualify you from living a more abundant life! Me and every other woman I know has had to heal or get delivered from some things. Sis, as long as you have life, chances are you will need to as well. I can't say this any clearer.

Undoubtedly you will have setbacks in life, but your past or present does NOT dictate your future. God designs your life, and then you decide how you will yield, cooperate, and participate in the plans that HE has designed for you!

Choose today to become unbreakable and move past the pit of pain to the place of productivity. Sisters, you can heal from your childhood trauma; you can heal from the abuse, from the betrayal, from the sin, from the addiction, and from whatever else there is in your life that has you broken, blocked and stuck!

GOD IS WITH YOU!!!!

Hear me on this…..GOD is with you!!! However, our bible teaches us the character of GOD, so we know that God is a gentleman. HE will not force a relationship with you. You must invite HIM to come in. However, when you do, when you finally allow the Holy Spirit to gain access to your broken places and damaged spaces, he will begin the work in you and through you!

That's why we must be unbreakable in your shit*uations*! If you ever get rooted in your faith, if you ever tap into your strengths, if you ever find the grit to push through, GOD will honor HIS promises for your life! I know it. It is biblical, and it is factual. Sure, things get rough, and life challenges are hard, but HE wants you to experience the abundant, plentiful, amazing life that He has planned for you, if only you believe.

Becoming unbreakable is going to require you to do your part. You will need to separate from people who crush your spirit or are destiny killers and dream stealers. Choose your tribe wisely and surround yourself with women of integrity, women who are supportive, honest, faithful and committed to seeing your growth.

Seek out healthy friendships, a mentor, a coach, a counselor, a therapist or perhaps a minister from church (pray and discern all relationships).

To sum it up, you are unbreakable when you become authentic as heck about who you truly are. There is freedom at this place. Be not ashamed of your weaknesses as the power of Christ work through you. You no longer need to show up in life as your representative. You are working through some stuff so stop pretending as though you have it all together. My friend once said to me, "I'm going to fake it till I make it." What!!! Seriously!!! No ma'am! Hecccccckkkk Nawwww!

Those days are over! Ladies, it's 2020, and WE ARE DONE faking it till we make it. We don't have time for this! We have kids to raise, businesses to build, classes to take, organizations to lead, new skills to learn, and homes to manage.

Stand firm, my sisters, and Level Up, Show Up and Evolve as authentic as you possibly can so that you won't have to fake anything. It is a beautiful thing when you get to make a difference in the world just by showing up as a new and improved YOU!

NOTES & IDEAS

20 LEVEL UP – CONCLUSION

GIRL, YOU ARE THE SH%T!

Phew, sister friends, we have come to the end of this book and the beginning of your journey of getting free. The Levolution has so many facets to it, but hopefully, I was able to highlight some key elements that will get you focused and moving onward and upward.

Before I go, I don't know who this is for, but I feel compelled to tell you to Forgive Yourself, Believe in Yourself, and Love Yourself!

You have been beating yourself up long enough. Let it go! Move on! And let's get to the business of building your Queendom! Beautiful lady, YOU ARE ENOUGH!

- Enough to make it through your Shit*uation*
- Enough to be in a healthy relationship
- Enough for the promotion
- Enough to start a business
- Enough to live an abundant
- Enough to have a happy love life

Everything that you need to make it in this life is already inside of you. Your gifts and talents that you have are ENOUGH to get you to your next level.

Every person on the planet has had and will need to Level Up and Evolve at some point in their life. So, The Levolution was created as a solution for doing just that.

Some women Level Up, and other women Level Up and Evolve. Ladies do both! By changing the mindset and believing that you can. And as I mentioned in the beginning, by going on your own personal mission to accomplish your goals and by seeing this as a movement for the rest of your life, a movement to – Level Up and Evolve!

Some days I struggle. Most days, I must still affirm my worth. But then again, no days will I ever stop investing in my growth and going after everything I work and pray for. The truth is, breaking free from past pain and getting unstuck is a process. Nevertheless, the hardest part of the process is where you start believing in YOURSELF and what GOD says about you!

As a Christ follower, I came to fully understand this truth of what God says about me, and my life changed instantly. What I mean by this is, I realized that I was either going to worry or I was going to worship. But I couldn't do both. So, what I am saying to you is this, Sisterfriends.....it's honesty time....it's time to tell some hard truths to yourself and others, and it's time to get your sh%t together! I will not allow you to wallow any longer. It's done! It's over! It happened, and you can't change a darn thing about it.

Coddling grown women is so 10 years ago. Go ahead and get in your last cry and then wipe those tears. Afterward, put on your best mascara and your favorite lipstick. Next, hold your head up high and look into your mirror and tell yourself – I GOT THIS! I am Beautiful, I am Brilliant, and I am Blessed!

You need to give yourself permission to be at peace with your past, the courage to embrace the process, and the tenacity to not let the hurdles stop your hustle.

Understand this, I gave myself permission. Permission to be me, as my most authentic self. Permission to live the abundant life promised to us as believers, permission to laugh and permission to love again. Whoa...... this one was a biggie!

Absolutely, I needed to allow myself to love again. I was hurt so badly in those past relationships that I had basically closed myself down to love. However, I knew that I wanted and needed love, and I desired to have it. Once I did the work to heal and forgive, love found me! Ironically, it found me at my most vulnerable, at my most needy and at my rawest. Yes, while I was going through my process, love found me.

I need you, ladies, to not miss this.... I was going through my process and love found me! (this is a praise break moment)

Once I changed my mindset and started the work to no longer

be broken, blocked and stuck, the universe said I will take it from here. GOD sent my husband.

We had known each other since our high school days but never really had a serious relationship. Through over 30 years, when I would be uncommitted in a relationship, he would pursue, we would lay and play, but we could never become officially official. When I was available and wanted more with him, he was committed or wild and free.

As the years would go by, Maxie will randomly pop up with a phone call or send a message through a mutual friend with words like – I will always love you, and one day, you will be my wife. He would get it in and then disappear, but no real chase to make me his. Therefore, I moved on and married "several" times before he realized that I was NOT going to wait around on him to "one day" make me his wife. Wouldn't you know, Maxie's one day came.

I was just getting out of the marriage with ex #2, and I had a dream about him one night, and in the dream, I was saying to my sister – *I am going to be okay. Maxie will take care of me. He always loved me.* The dream was so vivid. Would you believe, soon after having the dream, Maxie calls me? He said that he was just checking in to see how I was doing.

We had not been in communication for years, so I was shocked to receive his call. I told him that I was heading out to my friend's birthday party. He asked me where the party was and then insisted that it just so happens that he, too, was going to that same party.

Of course, I was nervous and excited that I would see him

after all of these years. Max walks into the party, greets me with a hug and then shortly after, he asks me if I would walk to his car with him. Okay, I agreed, but I was reluctant because I hadn't seen him in years.

We get to the car, and Maxie asks me to get inside of the car. I do! He asks me to open the glove box and pull out the folder that was inside. I do! At this point, I am thinking to myself, what the heck is wrong with him. He then goes on to instruct me to open the folder and read the papers inside. I did!

For all those years, Maxie would send me love letters that he would email me. When I married ex #2, I changed my email so the messages would return to him undeliverable. He had saved those emails and placed them into a folder because he said that "if he ever got a shot to be with me, he would have proof that he always loved me."

Excuse me as I pause here to wipe my tears.

His kind of love is what saved me from ME. It felt natural and genuine. I had never felt this level of love from ANY other man. For the first time in my life, I uncrossed my legs, unfolded my arms and closed my eyes. I exhaled.

Love for me has always been a battle. But this time, I was felt relieved from the duty of combat and realized that he was on my side and was not the enemy. I am no longer a prisoner of war. Though a casualty that was wounded in the battle, I survived. I escaped with wounds and a little PTSD, but I have adjusted to life just like the real war heroines and learned how to live with my scars. I am a survivor of the battles of life and love.

Though it was scary and unfamiliar territory, I did it. I

allowed myself to love and to be loved.

I am not saying that it has been easy. This man has years and years of a protected heart to penetrate. I thank GOD because he has been so patient with me as I learn this new skill and continue to let love have her way with me.

I am the woman I am today because of first GOD and then my husband, Maxie Graham. Loving and supporting me like he does makes it easy for me to become my best self.

I am whole – nothing missing and nothing lacking, and I attribute this to my Heavenly Father and the man that HE blessed me with. As I reflect on the thing that I am most grateful for in my life, it is experiencing unconditional love. The love from the birth of my girls filled the holes in my heart, and the love of GOD and my man sealed the cracks.

ABOUT THE AUTHOR – SHE IS THE SH%T

I AM THE SH%T

I am April D. Graham. I have worked for over twenty years with the Miami-Dade County Public Schools, where I started in the position of Teacher Assistant and worked my way to a school leader, Assistant Principal. As the first Assistant Principal appointed to Andover Middle School, I was exposed to a harsh reality—many girls and even female Teachers are lacking the tools needed to Win.

Surviving and not Thriving is NOT an option for me. Therefore, I made helping ladies my mission and birthed two mentoring organizations, America's Leading Ladies Leadership Academy (ALLLA) for girls and the Leadership Intern Training Executives (L.I.T.E.) for women aspiring to become administrators.

It was during my tenure at Andover that I recognized my gift for coaching ladies to shift their mindset from that of a victim to one of a victor! I had the gift of helping countless women to realize that it is possible to get unstuck and that they, too, can rewrite the narrative of their life.

My life was filled with sorrow and pain. I suffered abuse, neglect, rejection, and molestation, just to name a few of the hardships. I refused to surrender to my past and fought hard to nullify the prediction that was spoken over my life. I was constantly told I will never be anything and that I will always be on government assistance. However, my mission to become successful and a shift in my mindset prompted me to create a blueprint for my life that will ultimately lead me from an Ordinary me to an Extraordinary me. Yes, I am the sh%t! Because, against all odds, I leveled up and evolved. With GOD's guidance and my grit, I levolutionized myself.

In my mission to coach ladies to lead and soar through adversity, I established the America's Leading Ladies Academy, a nonprofit with the 501(c3) designation, and launched a coaching business. Through the Levolution Coaching Program, I offer personal support for ladies ready to reach their fullest potential.

I am a mindset coach dedicated to rewiring the way ladies who are stuck see themselves. My no-nonsense, no excuses, will not take no for an answer approach to helping ladies "break free" has empowered so many of them to become the very best versions of themselves.

I am the Leading Lady in my own hit movie. I have pushed through and persevered and earned four college degrees. I manage a successful childcare business and have earned a host of recognitions and distinctions in the field of education. Many who know me inquire about the possibility of my success when considering the odds that were stacked against me.

I did not have college-educated parents, causing me to become a first-generation college student.

With no positive role models and mentors throughout my life, I struggled financially my entire childhood and early adulthood, had no support and even fewer resources. Yet, I was able to attain some level of "success."

I am married to my dream. I birthed two beautiful daughters and have two handsome nephews whom I adore and love dearly.

I am A LEADER, I AM A BELIEVER, and my mindset is that I will either win or learn.

Either way, It will always be a WIN-WIN for me!